AKALI PHULA SINGH

WHY HE IS KNOWN AS THE 'PROTECTOR OF THE SIKH FAITH'?

ISHWAR SINGH

Copyright © Ishwar Singh
All Rights Reserved.

This book has been published with all efforts taken to make the material error-free after the consent of the author. However, the author and the publisher do not assume and hereby disclaim any liability to any party for any loss, damage, or disruption caused by errors or omissions, whether such errors or omissions result from negligence, accident, or any other cause.

While every effort has been made to avoid any mistake or omission, this publication is being sold on the condition and understanding that neither the author nor the publishers or printers would be liable in any manner to any person by reason of any mistake or omission in this publication or for any action taken or omitted to be taken or advice rendered or accepted on the basis of this work. For any defect in printing or binding the publishers will be liable only to replace the defective copy by another copy of this work then available.

Contents

Preface

This book is about the brief history of **Akali Phula Singh**. The task behind to publish such content is to spread knowledge about the unsung heroes of the Sikh history among the new generation. In the schools, which are being organised by Sikh trusts, the students are just getting very limited knowledge about the Sikh warriors. Baba Banda Singh Bahadur, Baba Deep Singh, Hari Singh Nalua etc. are the common names on the tongues of the students but they don't know about the others. This is just an effort to spread this brief information among new generations.

Acknowledgements

I would like to thanks SikhiWiki, the Encyclomedia of Sikhs for providing free data about the Sikh history. A web based encyclopaedia of the Sikh Way of Life written collaboratively by many of its readers. It is a great place to learn about Sikhi and the message of the 11 Gurus.

CHAPTER ONE

INTRODUCTION

Akali Baba Phula Singh was born January 14, 1761 in the village of Sarinh, In the present day district of Sangrur Punjab. In to a Jatt family of Sarao clan, His father, Baba Ishar Singh of Misal Shaheedan, was seriously wounded in the Wadda Ghalughara (the Great Holocaust) of 1762, and died shortly thereafter. Deeply religious from early childhood, Akali Phula Singh joined the Jatha of Akali Baba Naina Singh ji, Misal Shaheedan and started living with Babaji. Misal Shaheedan was the Dal of Baba Deep Singh ji Shaheed, Jatha of dedicated Gursikhs who had a highly spiritual life and lived life according to true Gurmat principles. This was the first Jatha to be given a Nishan (a Flag) and a Nagara (a Battle Drum) when the Khalsa Panth was organized into five jathas in 1734. Its duty was to look after Gurudwaras and Takhats, give Gurbaani vidya, Shastarvidya and Naam Abhyaas. The Sixth Jathedar of Misal Shaheedan, Akali Baba Naina Singh ji lived at Sri Amritsar Sahib most of the time. Baba Phula Singh ji also started living at the Harimandir at an early age in a sangath of Gursikhs that included Baba Naina Singh ji and Giani Bhai Soorat Singh ji, who was the head granthi of Sri Darbar Sahib. In no time he was well trained in Gurbaani Vidya and all the martial arts and ended up becoming the leader of the devout band of fearless fighters.

Nihangs (the order of Santly Warriors created by Dasam Pita Guru Gobind Singh ji, to serve and protect the Khalsa Community) have always been renowned for their martial skills, their daredevil courage, as well as, their willingness to speak their minds. Many historians have refered to the Nihang units as "Suicide squads". This assumpsion is utterly wrong, for suicide is considered a sin in the Sikh religion. It is easy, however, to see why the word suicide has been used, because the attacks of the Sikh Nihangs (the word Nihang, is said to be derived from Persian, meaning crocodile) were so similar to the swift attack the crocodile launches upon any unsuspecting being who wanders too near a peacefull river's edge - an attack launched with little thought of their own safety, full of wild, thrashing fury which ends only when their prey is subdued. It is interesting that while the Persian word crocodile is often used to explain the name Nihang that the Punjabi word niching, meaning outspoken, unhesitating, without doubt and bold applies to the qualities of the Nihangs as well. Like the often asked question; which came first, the egg or the chicken, one wonders if the word nishang preceded the Nihangs or vice versa.

Generally Nihangs never marry, their only purpose being to live and, if needed, to die in defence of the Khalsa. There have been many warriors who were true to the high symbol and unflinching will, of the Khalsa. Unfortunately, there were also many who joined the Khalsa for personal glory or to win jagirs (estates), but if we look to find a man whose one and only purpose in becoming a Nihang was to serve the Khalsa and to keep the Nishan Sahib flying high, then that one man could only be - Nihang Akali Phula

Singh.

CHAPTER TWO

NIHANGAN DI CHAWONI

Holding to tradition Akali Phula Singh never married. He settled down in Amritsar, where, today, a burj (tower) and a dera (temple) called Nihangan di Chawoni (Camp of the Nihangs) still stands in his memory. As a child 'Baba Ji' decided to dedicate his life to the care of Sikh shrines. He loved to serve people in accordance with the Guru's message. Later, when he was 18 years old he shifted to the fort of Gobindgarh where he became a leader of one of the bands of fighters (a squad) of the Sikh army. When Maharaja Ranjit Singh sought to make Amritsar part of Khalsa Raj he first laid siege to the city. When Akali Phula Singh saw the forces of the Bhangi Misls (then in control of Amritsar), preparing to face their fellow Sikhs Akali Phula Singh, with some leading citizens of the city, bravely put themselves in harms way, between the opposing forces. Adressing each group, he spoke of the futility and senselessness of Sikhs spilling each others' blood. Peace and reconsiliation was chosen and the Bhangi chieftans each surrendered their share of Amritsar into the Maharaja's hands. Akali Phula Singh joined the Maharaja's army along with 3,000 Nihangs. For his many efforts he was made the Jathedar of the Akal Takht in 1807.

A born leader, who lived his life in accordance with the moral codes of the Sikh Gurus, he even called Maharaja Ranjit Singh to task, when he married outside of the Sikh fold (he had married a Muslim woman, named Moran of Lahore). As the Jathedar of the Akal Takth, Akali Phula Singh, declared that Maharaja Ranjit singh was no longer a Sikh, declaring him to be a Tankhaiya (removed from the Sikh fold). He issued a Huknama, ordering the Maharaja to appear before the Sikh Sangat, in front of the Akal Takht (a tradition begun by Guru Hargobind that has been followed to this day.) To his credit, the mighty Maharaja answered the Huknama (order) of Akali Phula Singh. The humbled Ranjit Singh admitted that he had made a mistake. Akali Phula Singh then ordered a punishment of 50 lashes for Maharaja Ranjit Singh to be carried out immediately.

Ranjit Singh took off his shirt and bowed down to receive his punishment, seeing this Akali Phula Singh asked the Community (Sadh Sangat) to forgive the Maharaja for this mistake. And thus the Maharaja was pardoned, but not before he promised that he would not marry again. Maharaja Ranjit Singh who loved and respected the Harmandir and the Akal Takht, unlike many other monarchs of the World, never tried to replace Akali Phula Singh as Jathedar, remaining true to the authority he had invested in Akali Phula Singh.

Ranjit Singh donated the Gold with which the Muslim artisans of Amritsar clad the copper sheathing of the upper portions of the Harmandir Sahib, giving the Harimandir Sahib its modern popular name - the Golden Temple.

There is another interesting incident of that time ended in the Maharaja deciding to modernize and reform his forces along the lines of the British army. On the day of Muharram in February 25, 1809, a mostly Shia Muslim unit of the British army, under the command of General Metcalf (a British officer) was visiting Amritsar. The Shias, apparently Metcalf was elsewhere, decided to undertake a traditional Muharram procession through the streets of Amritsar, even though the majority of Amritsar's Muslims were Sunnis who felt (then as now) that the Shia processions were sacrilege. But that day it would not be the usual blood letting between Muslims that occured.

It also happened to be the day of Holi, when the Nihangs were celebrating Hola Mohalla along with their celebrated leader the Jathedar of the Akal Takth, Akali Phula singh. As the Shia procession worked its way through the twisting streets of Amritsar, beating their breasts to the loud chants of "Hasan, Hussein, Ali", they paused in front of the Golden Temple, where the Akalis were then in prayer. The Akalis remonstrated with the processionists to go elsewhere. Arguments led to a scuffle and the Shia Sepoys of General Metcaulfe came to a head on collision with the Akalis.

It is not known who elevated the arguments to a bloody riot. Even General Metcalfe was doubtful and conceded that the first shot was probably fired by one of his Shia escorts (Metcalfe No. 72, of 7.3.1809). In total there were about 50 casualties on both sides. In the end the riot was stopped when Ranjit Singh, who had come to the city for the festivities, personally came forward and helped to quell the fighting. With peace again restored he went to Metcalfe and apologized for the riot. Ranjit Singh was most impressed by the discipline shown by the Shia Sepoys, who snapped back into their formation and stopped fighting , as Metcalfe had commanded. The Maharaja promptly decided to modernize his Army along the lines of the British forces.

It was not long before experienced officers, out of jobs after the recent Napoleanic Wars, became the first of many Europeans, seeking to 'find' their fortunes, under the Maharaja's command.

Akali Phula Singh and the Modernization of the Khalsa

Akali Phula Singh walking through the fields with his horse, by artist Kanwar Singh.

Akali Phula Singh was against the Europeanization of the Khalsa Forces. He believed more in the fighting qualities of Khalsa blessed by Guru Gobind Singh. Ranjit Singh was a statesman who foresaw that he could utilize a well disciplined army to subdue the whole of Punjab and to face the British if it ever came to it. Then in the same year of 1809, at Ropar, Maharaja Ranjit Singh signed a treaty with the British recognizing the river Satluj as a permanent border between the Sarkar Khalsa and the British. Akali Phula Singh wanted the Maharaja to tear up and discard the treaty. He even threatened to quit. Maharaja Ranjit Singh explained to him that first they would subdue the whole of the Punjab, and then later they would confront the British.

The Maharaja was well ahead of his times in taking this decision, a decision which soon rendered him as the only ruler in all of Asia who could stand toe to toe with the British. He effectively ended their westward advance across India. It would be another quarter century before the Japanese Ruler saw the necessity of modernizing his forces to stop the colonial advances of the industrialized European Armies. And as in the case with Ranjit Singh and Akali Phula Singh the Emperor of Japan had to overcome the objections of his Samurai's who resisted the new ways of war out of loyalty to their warriors code and tried and true ways.

Akali Phula Singh and his command helped Maharaja in the campaigns of Kasur, Multan, and others waged all over the Punjab. Nihangs under his command at Multan surpassed all bravery when they bowed down one by one to support one side of a Gun being used to break through the fort and attained martyrdom. By 1822 all the regiments of the Sarkar Khalsa were modernized along the lines of the European armies. Akali Phula Singh was given new arms and trained in new tactics by the former French General Ventura a veteran of the Napoleanic Wars.

In 1815 Maharaja Ranjit Singh decided to turn his conquests towards the North West Frontier provinces. He took control of a number of principalities making them tributories to the Khalsa Kingdom. For 10 centuries the Pathans and other tribesman of the northwest had thundered out of their hills and plundered the Punjab and India, this was the first time that any Punjabi had taken the battle to the raiders' homes. When in 1823, the Governor of Peshawar failed to profer the agreed upon tribute to Maharaja Ranjit Singh the Sarkar Khalsa forces, led by Akali Phula Singh, General Hari Singh Nalwa, Fateh Singh Attariwala, and Prince Sher Singh and of course the Maharaja advanced towards Peshawar.

CHAPTER THREE

BATTLE OF NAUSHERA

The Battle of Naushera in 1823 AD, in which thousands were killed was fought with the Pathans tribes of the Yusufzais, Khattaks and Afridis. Prince Sher Singh and Hari Singh Nalwa led the advance columns early in 1823. They spanned the river Attock by the means of a pontoon bridge and occupied the fort of Jehangiria. Then Maharaja Ranjit singh along with Akali Phula Singh led the remainder of the Khalsa forces upto the Eastern bank of the River Attock. By this time the Pathani tribes had destroyed the pontoon bridge and besieged Prince Sher Singh and Hari Singh Nalua in the fortof Jehangiria. Hastingly, Maharaja Ranjit Singh, who had crossed the river many times before, forged it again coming to the rescue of his son Prince Sher Singh, Hari Singh Nalwa and their embattled forces just in time.

The Khattaks and Yusufzais were pushed back and managed to entrench themselves on an eminence called Pir Sabak or Tibbi Tiri on the plains between Jehangiria and Peshawar. The main Afghan force under Azim Khan's brother was separated from the tribal ghazis by a small but swift-running stream, the Landai. The Khalsa Artillery, led by Mian Ghausa bypassed the tribesmen, and reached the bank of the Landai, and training its heavy guns on the opposite bank. Azim Khan made a dash from Peshawar and joined the Afghan forces on the opposite Bank of the Landai. He could not cross the stream due to the heavy bombardment by the Khalsa forces from their side of the Landai.

On the other war front, the Sarkar Khalsa launched an offensive at Pir Sabak Hill. The Khalsa forces were heavily outnumbered by the Afghans, but the Khalsa forces evened the odds by the tactics of their now well trained, disciplined army. The Tribal forces fought desperately but were overcome by the Sarkar Khalsa's Gurkhas and Mussalman Najibs. Then Akali Phula Singh and his Nihangs moved up to give them the coup de grace as their french General had probably remarked. They drove the Khattaks and Yusufzais before them leaving four thousand Afghans dead and dying on the field. It is said that they ran from their Nihang attackers saying:

"Toba, toba-, Khuda Khud, Khalsa Shud"

God forbid, it's as if, God himself has become a Khalsa (Nihang)

Mohammed Azim Khan retreated to Peshawar. He was too ashamed to face his people and thus he returned to Afghanistan and died soon.

Even though the Sarkar Khalsa had paid a heavy price with the death of a great warrior like Akali Phula Singh, it proved a crushing defeat for the Afghans, which convinced the Pathan tribesmen of the superiority of Punjabi soldiers. Three days later the Maharaja entered Peshawar at the head of his victorious troops. The citizens welcomed him and paid homage with nazaranas (monetary tributes).

CHAPTER FOUR

More on Akali Phoola Singh

The great Sikh General, Jathedar Akali Phoola Singh, was born in 1761. His father Ishar Singh was fatally wounded during the great massacre of Sikhs (Wada Ghalughara) in 1762. Before his death he charged Bhai Narain Singh of Misl Shaheedan with the responsibility of raising his infant son.

Akali Ji, by the age of ten, could recite Nitnem and other Gurbani hymns. At Anandpur Sahib, he always kept himself busy doing sewa or reading Gurbani, and he became very popular with the sangat. Because of his scholastic attitude and commitment to Panthic welfare, he was made the leader (Jathedar) of the Misl after the death of Bhai Narain Singh. In 1800, he came to Amritsar and made the Mahants improve the management of the Gurdwaras. The major credit for extending the boundaries of the Sikh Raj goes to Akali Ji, the legendary general of the Sikhs.

CHAPTER FIVE

RESPECTED BY MAHARAJA RANJIT SINGH

1802, Maharaja Ranjit Singh sent his army to Amritsar, which he planned to annex to his kingdom. Akali Phoola Singh suggested that the Maharaja give an estate to the Bhangi Misl, then ruling Amritsar. The army was ordered not to loot the inhabitants of the city.

1807, Phoola Singh was, for the first time, involved in a major battle against the Nawab of Kasoor, who had the protection of a strong fort. The Sikhs fought bravely and were finally able to demolish a section of the wall. The Nawab was arrested. The Maharaja took pity on him and allotted him an estate near the Sutlej river. The bravery of Akali Ji during the battle very much impressed the Maharaja.

1808, a British representative was sent to Amritsar for the purpose of developing better relations between the two governments. During the visit, some Muslim soldiers (part of the British platoon that had escorted the British emissary) took out a procession in celebration of one of their festivals. It wasn't long before they began chanting loudly, but as they approached the Akal Takhat some Sikhs asked them to stop yelling, because it would disturb the Sikh congregation. However, the leaders of the procession insulted the Sikhs instead of listening to their suggestion. Being told of this, Akali Ji went to settle the matter with the British Commander. The soldiers apologized and behaved respectfully in the future, after that things remained peaceful near the Harmandar Sahib.

CHAPTER SIX

LOSS OF FAITH IN THE MAHARAJA

The internal political policy pursued by Maharaja Ranjeet Singh went against Sikh interests. Major points of differences were that the Maharaja had:

1. Delegated too much authority of the government to Dogras who were insincere and disloyal to the Sikhs.

2. Appointed relatives of his cronies to important posts instead of selecting competent persons.

3. Developed misunderstanding with his sons by listening to the misinformation given by the Dogras.

Note: Later, it was found that Akali Ji was right and justified in asking the Maharaja not to place all his confidence in the Dogras alone. The Dogras had a secret understanding with the British, who had already taken control over much of India. The Dogras caused the downfall of the Sikh Raj. They were made the rajas of Kashmir as a reward for helping the British infiltrate the Sikh raj. The Dogras also informed the Kabul regime about the Sikh army and they planned the murder of the hero of the Sikh raj, Sardar Hari Singh Nalwa, who was considered a terror by the Afghans and Pathans.

When Akali Phoola Singh Ji went to discuss domestic policies of the government with Maharaja Ranjeet Singh, the Dogras did not allow the meeting to take place. Akali Ji forced his entry into the palace and was warmly received by the Maharaja. Showing his hospitality, the Maharaja offered Akali Ji a splendid meal. Akali Ji declined his offer stating that unless the Maharaja changed his policies, and realized his own entrapment by the Dogras, this was to be their last meeting. After delivering this message to the Maharaja, Akali Ji left for Anandpur Sahib.

The Prince of Jind state (Jind was then part of the British Raj, now a part of the Haryana state of India.) developed differences with the British raj. He moved to Anandpur Sahib and took protection under Akali Ji. The British desired the Prince to be handed over to them. They approached the Maharaja when Akali Ji refused to surrender him to them. The Dogras misinformed and misguided the Maharaja and accused Akali Ji of creating enmity between the British and the Sikh raj. The army at Phillaur was, therefore, instructed to arrest Akali Phoola Singh. The army, however, declined to obey the Maharaja recognizing that Akali Ji was the holiest man amongst the Sikhs.

The British also tried to capture Akali Ji by ordering the Nawab of Malerkotla and Raja Jaswant to attack Anandpur Sahib and arrest Akali Ji along with the Prince of Jind. Both of them knew of Phoola Singh's goodness and greatness. They also endorsed his stand and refused to cooperate with the British. Finally, Maharaja Ranjeet Singh thought of another plan to get Akali Ji on his side. He sent Baba Sahib Singh Bedi, a close friend of Akali Phoola Singh, to escort him with honor to Amritsar where a spectacular welcome was arranged by the Maharaja. The two were finally reconciled. Unfortunately, the Maharaja did not take advantage of his advice to keep the Dogras away from the helm of administration.

CHAPTER SEVEN

PROTECTOR OF THE SIKH FAITH

Some administrators of the Kashmir area broke their agreement. Akali Phoola Singh and General Hari Singh were sent to punish them. In 1816, Akali Ji lead his forces against the rebels in the west and south of Punjab, including the Nawab of Multan who had not paid his taxes. In 1817, Phoola Singh was sent to Hazara to recover the taxes. The administrator paid his dues and was, therefore, allowed to continue in his position by Akali Ji.

The Nawab of Multan again declined to pay his taxes to the state. When the army was sent to collect the dues, he defeated the Lahore army. The Maharaja then sent his son with a strong force who pushed the Nawab into the fort, but could not achieve his mission. At last, the Maharaja came to Amritsar and humbly requested Akali Phoola Singh to help the Khalsa Panth. Akali Ji angrily asked: "O supporter of the disloyal Dogras, why did you not tell me earlier?" Akali Ji took his men to Multan. They demolished the wall of the fort. A bloody hand to hand battle followed. The brave Nawab, his five sons and 12,000 soldiers lost their lives in the battle. Akali Ji was wounded. On his return to Amritsar,

Akali Ji was honored and given the title "Protector of the Sikh Faith."

CHAPTER EIGHT

BATTLES FOR PESHAWAR

In 1818, the Maharaja himself led the expedition to bring the rebellious Pathans under control. A pontoon bridge was constructed across the river Attock and a small Jatha was sent to assess the situation, but it was attacked. This enraged the Maharaja. He sent Akali Phoola Singh and general Hari Singh Nalwa against the rebels. As soon as the Sikh army was within firing range, they were showered with a rain of bullets. Akali Ji ordered a tactical retreat. This made the rebels come out of their bunkers to follow the retreating Sikhs and push them out of their area. When the enemy was in the open battlefield, Akali Ji ordered a severe attack and then encircled them. Their commander Feroze Khan accepted his defeat and requested the Sikhs to end the battle.

The next target of the Sikh army was to retrieve the control of Peshawar. The rebels decided to obstruct their path to the city. When Akali Ji was informed about this he immediately attacked them before they could gather and organize a coordinated resistance to his advance to Peshawar. This strategy proved useful. The Ghazis (Muslim fighters) did not dare to face the Sikhs and ran for their lives. The road was left open for the Sikhs to proceed to the city where they raised their flag on the fort. After the Sikhs took control of Peshawar, Yar Mohammed Khan sent gifts to Maharaja Ranjeet Singh to express his loyalty. The Maharaja accepted the gifts and made him the Governor of Peshawar. But Khan, too, proved disloyal to the Sikh raj.

CHAPTER NINE

BATTLES FOR KASHMIR

In 1819 Akali Ji was deputed to discipline the ruler of Kashmir who had broken the agreement made with the Maharaja. Unable to proceed through the Pass protected by the army, the Sikhs were instructed to follow footpaths through hilly terrain. By this tactical move they took over all the outer defense posts without much difficulty. After heavy fighting, they captured the strong fort as well.

The Sikh army was unable to make further progress, as the route to Pir Panchal Pass was blocked by the Pathans. The Pathans, occupying the sides of the path, rained bullets on the Sikh army. Akali Ji directed his soldiers to get on the mountains, instead of moving through the Pass. The Sikhs fought the Pathans hand-to-hand and continued their journey through the Pass.

The next battle took place with Jabar Khan, who had built a strong army with thousands of Afghans. Diwan Chand ordered the Sikh army to open gun fire on Afghan positions, but it did little harm to them. He then directed his men to advance their guns to get closer to the defenses for effective firing. As soon as the Sikhs stopped firing in order to move their guns, the Afghans came out of their bunkers and attacked them, capturing several Sikh guns.

Finding the Afghans in the open battlefield, Akali Ji responded with a lightning attack by his men, who were considered the best swordsmen. Jabar Khan was wounded and he fled. The Khalsa won the battle and took control of the Kashmir state.

CHAPTER TEN

DEFEATING KABUL FORCES

In 1823, Mohammed Azim Khan, the ruler of Kabul, made plans to take over Peshawar. Yar Mohd Khan, the Governor of Peshawar, appointed by Maharaja Ranjeet Singh was his brother. He agreed to help the Kabul regime by withdrawing from the city and leaving it unoccupied. The Khan's army came and occupied the city without firing a single bullet. Local administrators and communities were instigated to rebel against the Sikh raj. They occupied all the routes to Peshawar making it very dangerous for the Sikh army to go there.

When this news reached Lahore, the Maharaja called General Hari Singh Nalwa and sought his advice. He suggested that Akali Phoola Singh must join him to recover the state from Khan. Nalwa immediately left for Peshawar, with the Maharaja and Akali Ji following him. When they reached Attock, they found that the pontoon bridge had been destroyed to stop the Sikhs from crossing the river and helping Nalwa.

General Nalwa and his forces were engaged in a bloody battle on the western side of the river while the Maharaja and the main Sikh army were delayed on the eastern bank. Hearing the fight across the river, the Sikhs became more worried and distressed at their situation. A messenger, who swam across the river, informed Akali Phoola Singh and the Maharaja that unless Nalwa and his soldiers received help, he would most likely lose the battle. Hearing this, Akali Phoola Singh got on his horse and crossed the river followed by the Maharaja and the rest of the forces. The news of the arrival of the Maharaja demoralized the opponents and they lost all hope of winning the battle. They ran to save their lives and took shelter behind their second defense line, Nawshehra fort, to prepare a strong defense.

After reorganizing their forces, the Sikhs decided to move forward to take over the fort. Having said their prayers, the Jathas started marching, when a scout brought the news that a new army of 10,000 men with forty guns had arrived to support the rebels. The Maharaja wanted to wait for their own guns to arrive but Akali Ji said, "The Khalsa has started its march after prayer, now no one can stop them!"

When the Sikh army was within their range, the Ghazis opened fire on the Sikhs. Akali Ji ordered them to move forward suddenly and engage them in hand to hand combat, an art in which no army could match the Khalsa. Bullets were coming from all sides, but Akali Ji was moving forward with his men. His horse was killed by a bullet. He immediately boarded an elephant to continue his advance on the Ghazis. Watching the daring deeds of the Akali platoons, the Maharaja could not resist joining them. Meanwhile the Akali men had reached the firing lines and started fighting with their swords. The Afghans were no match for the quick swords of the Sikhs. Fresh Sikh army

and gunmen also reached the battlefield by that time and
the Sikhs claimed another victory.

CHAPTER ELEVEN

THE SIKH NATION BEREAVED

Unfortunately, the Sikhs sustained a grievous wound: the death of Akali Phoola Singh. A Pathan, hiding behind a boulder, shot Akali Ji from close range as he was pressing the Pathans to retreat. Thus, the Sikhs lost their great General, a true Sikh. He was a fearless and skilled commander. He maintained the Sant-Sipahi (Saint-Soldier) tradition of the Khalsa. Akali Phoola Singh Ji remains a role model for all Sikhs.

References

"The Heritage of the Sikhs" by Sardar Harbans Singh, ISBN 81-7304-064-8

"Umdat-ut-twarikh" by Sohan Lal Suri

"History of Sikhs" Part 1 and Part 2 by Khushwant Singh